# My Inside Opened Out

## Patricia Flowers

To Lawrence

love from

Pat
x

keep the poems coming .

William Cornelius Harris Publishing

In collaboration
with
London Poetry Books

ISBN 978-1-911232-38-4

14 Fairlawn 159 Kingsway Hove

London Poetry Books

# To Guy

who heard me

And with thanks to Survivors Poetry and Paper Tiger for welcoming me into their communities of poets and performers, especially for the encouragement of Debbie Macnamara, Dave Russell, Jason Why and Keith Bray.

I have loved poetry all my life: read it, recited it, quoted it, taught it, analysed it, encouraged pupils and family members to write it… Finally, at the beginning of 2020, the deposit of many years came pouring out of me, with the lockdown that soon followed giving ample opportunity for development. Here are my poems, from the first beginnings, exploring my experiences of: nature; life, love and loss; therapy; and faith.

Cover artwork by Patricia Flowers

# Contents

# MY INSIDE OPENED OUT

# Seen

Fingers feeling a face
to trace contours
intimately shaped:
that nose, those eyes, those lips ...
To gaze in wonder
with enjoyment
into another soul.

This look a fountain of life,
a fountain of grace,
the security of the soul,
the beginning of learning.

These shapes the templates
against which to shape the world,
the bedrock of the heart,
a calibration.

# Poetry: My Manifesto

I finally found my voice,
It built up inside till I had no choice,
It makes me cry and it makes me rejoice.
I want to get up and go with it,
Feel it and flow with it,
Grab, grasp and grow with it.
I'm gonna dance with it,
Fall into a trance with it,
Entertain my nieces and my aunts with it,
Express everything God grants with it.

I want to celebrate the anniversaries,
Annihilate the adversaries,
Cut down and cut out the curse-aries,
Experiment with the verse-aries,
Laugh with it,
Graft with it,
Craft with it.
I want to play with it,
Have a great day with it,
Know what to say with it.
I'm gonna roll with it,
Fill up my soul with it,
Make myself whole with it.

I want to
Gently, tentatively,
Doubtfully, inquisitively,
Persistently, positively,
Courageously, compassionately, creatively
Engage with it,
Climb out of my cage with it,
Become seer and sage with it,
Express fear and rage with it.
I'm gonna spill my guts with it,
Pose and strut with it,
Get out of my rut with it,
Get up off my butt with it.
I want to change the world with it,
Tell myself, 'Go, girl!' with it,
Let my banner unfurl with it.

Man, I'm gonna
Live in it, live on it,
Live it up with it,
Live it out with it,
Shout with it,
Until the last whisper
Leaves my lips.

# Have You Seen Grass Grow?

'All flesh is grass,' the prophets cry,
'Here today and tomorrow thrown into the fire,'
Symbol of mutability,
Transience personified; an image of our tiny life,
A speck on the vast expanse of long eternity
But ...
Have you seen grass grow?

Where have you seen a blade?
Pushing through tarmac? Have you spent an hour
Tugging out grass from in between the stones
That pave your garden path?
Seen it on walls, in every crack and crevice?
Clinging to cliffs in careless tufts,
Coming from nowhere into the
New concrete city development?
Yes, have you seen grass grow?

Pulled it from the flowerbed,
Excavating every root (or so you thought)
Because just next weekend ...
Have you seen grass grow?

'Grass roots,' they say, 'a grass roots movement,
More powerful than a mighty tyrant,'
Because grass roots are hardy,
Persistent and ubiquitous,
Meaning everywhere, pervasive, difficult to find
And separate.

And what about a lawn?
How keen is grass to separate itself,
To be pedigree, unmixed, exclusive, pure?
It welcomes in the clover and the moss,
The buttercups and daisies, dandelions and thistles,
Living alongside, entangled, embracing, inclusive.
Grass does not discriminate.
Sorry, you lovers of lawns, it will take all your time,
Your effort and your strength to bend the grass
To your controlling will, but look away
For just one minute – just relax your grip –
And ...
Have you seen grass grow?

The seeds are tiny – who could sift each one
Out of their endless garden soil?
And even if you could, how soon would lawn
Blow back its babies into the flowerbed,
Riding on the breeze?
Yes, have you seen grass grow?
I don't think grass will become extinct
Any time soon.

And so the strong and fragile grass
Of human life goes on,
Cut down in a moment by cancer or catastrophe,
Collision with a double decker bus,
But ...
Have you seen life grow?
Grow like a blade of grass in a pinprick of dust
In the middle of a demolition site?
How did it get there?

In the war zone, in the blighted city,
From the flood plain of Bangladesh
To the wildfires of Australia and California,
People, children even, uprooted, detached,
Cast out and blown away, separated,
Reach out for somewhere ... anywhere ...
To send out roots and shoots, to begin to live again.

And even as I write, somewhere inside me
A seed in the desert dust of a desolate waste
Smells moisture in the air, feels the sun's warmth,
Splits, cracks, lets out a microscopic shoot
Feeling in the dark for somewhere to attach and make a home,
To cling precariously to such moorings as are left,
To let life grow and flow in these unlikely places,
Because life, like grass, is not choosy.
It only wants to grow ...
And have you seen grass grow?

# The Trees in Spring

Our winter shapes support us: what is left
After long winter shakes and strips the leaves,
Each rotting branch and disconnected twig
Torn off by tempest wild or boist'rous breeze.
Stripped to the form defining us we stand,
The trunk well set, the branches fixed just so,
Sending a delicate tracery of twigs
Towards the sky, while roots reach out below.
Repeated onslaughts of the winter's waste
Have made us what we are, revealed our shape,
But now the rotted refuse of our days
Feeds life into our roots, to rise in sap
And clothe us once again in tender green
Till life from last year's loss again is seen.

# First Leaves

This green that the camera can't capture
And maybe neither can my words:
Vibrant – too strong; new – too old;
Young – too human; fresh – too vegetable;
Newborn – but not helpless;
Virginal – yet fecund.

A first unveiling of leaves,
Forming a veil that softens
The stark shapes of the trees,
A gauzy gown worn by a tender debutante,
Innocent, wide-eyed, shy and strong,
Full not so much of life but of the promise of life.

A green not found in any paintbox
Nor captured by the brushstrokes of my pen,
Only to be seen and drunk in by the eyes,
An indescribable blessing,
Conferring hope and beauty.
And springtime. And life.

# Nature's Imperatives

Imperatives of growth and healing
Hardwired into creation ...

I have watched these trees
All summer, skeletons at first,
Then clothed in pale green draperies,
Darkening and thickening, becoming weighty,
Their whispers in the wind
Grown to a full-voiced cadence,
Like the surging of sea-waves:
Music that soothes my soul.

In April I penned an ode
To the first green leaves of spring,
A green that prompted wonder
I barely could describe,
And now in every shade of green
Leaves frame the woodland path,
Strung like so many lanterns
Glinting in the sun.

Take the light away,
Send the sun behind a cloud,
And the path loses all magic,
Prosaic again, and dusty.
But light it up once more,
And dust motes dance like glitter,
The very air a-dazzle
With incandescent life.

Walking back across the common,
Constellations of tiny dandelions
Sprinkle the dry grass,
Emitting light like stars,
While a quieter brightness
Shimmers on the water
Where the ducks drift slowly,
Mirrored, in the midday heat.

Back home the pumpkin plant
Continues its takeover of the lawn,
The span of leaves extending,
A saucer's width across,
A tea-plate, then a dinner-plate,
And now a serving platter,
Visibly, tangibly,
Increasing every day.

Imperatives of creation
Stir also in my heart:
Words, pictures, music
Form and grow unbidden,
Imperceptibly driven,
As shapes which have been hidden
Crystallise apart,
And swell into their fullness.

The growth of creativity
In my deserted soul,
As a new garden
Planted in waste land.
After the shudder of the tractor,
The depth of digging,
The clearing, the sifting,
The planting and the tending ...

Creativity's imperatives
Of healing and growth.

# Seasons

Spring burst with joy and freshness,
With excitement and promise:
Bare shapes of trees
Clothed delicately,
Then leaves upon leaves
Forming full, rich, green swells
Of summer, heavy and hot,
Maturing and fruiting.
And to release that fruit
Something has had to fall,
Something has had to break,
Something has had to die.
And now, as leaves dry and thin,
Here is that shape again
Beginning to emerge:
The dry leaves first
Display their loveliest colours;
The mature tree lets them fall,
Trusting in life,
Content to let them go,
Understanding loss
Better than before,
Ready to be sad and stark,
Loving its own authentic shape
And its nurturing, overwintering heart,
Deep rooted in the ground,
Knowing beyond a doubt
That it is safe, and sound.

# Consider the Lilies of the Field

Considering (as instructed) the lilies
And the other garden plants,
Both flowers and veg,
I asked myself,
'Today, what did they do?'
They grew.

I've seen it:
Tiny green tomatoes
Forming in a row,
Pumpkin leaves
Visibly broader,
Gladioli
Getting taller,
Cabbages expanding
To fill the border;
That's what they do.
They grow.

And for all my efforts today,
What have I got to show?

# Christmas Day 2020

My boots paddle and splash
On the puddled path;
Mallards and gulls, moorhens and coots
Glide gracefully.
Sun shines through the branches
I have been watching all year
In their rolling cavalcade
Of colour and shape and form.
Here is the place I have followed the seasons,
Taking them in like never before,
Feeding on filtered sunlight,
The wind, the rain, dryness, wetness,
On peacefulness
That permeates my core.
Here are the families playing,
Friends meeting on park benches,
Merry Christmas greetings to those we pass.
2020 – the year Christmas was cancelled.
2020 – the year we found
Our home in the outdoors.

# Go, Nature, Sing!

Go, Nature, sing!
A bit of sunshine
And it's party time.
A palm tree
With its stiff leaves
Staccato clackers
A pair of maracas,
A birdsong cacophony
Makes full polyphony,
The ground squelching,
A sponge belching
Its surfeit of rain
Which it drunk
Again and again,
Swimming away,
Creating the bass line
For party time
In the sunshine.

Go, Nature, sing!
I think it'll take
Until spring
For the trees
To clap their hands and sing,
A Biblical injunction
That needs leaves to function,
For now the wind's hustle
Achieves just a faint rustle,
But the parakeet's shriek
Challenges beak
And throat to competition,
From every direction
A strident repetition
Of each one's motif,
Vying for chief
Performer.
And yet there is order.

Go, Nature, sing!
A bit of sunshine
And it's party time.

**Government Guidance** for the public on the mental health and wellbeing aspects of coronavirus: If you can, get outside. If you can't, bring nature in.

Today I let trills of birdsong
into my head,
rivulets and rills of sound
washing away the inner dialogue
of a busy mind,
the fruitless search for a script
I waste my time
trying to find.
All the air was filled with singing,
quadraphonic surround sound,
like that time they hid
the trumpets in the gallery
and woodwinds in the wings,
music rising from every direction
all around.

Today I opened my eyes wide,
took a headlong dive
into the infinite blue of the sky,
sight tracing the silhouettes of trees,
riding on cloudy puffs of grey and white,
coming back to earth
to rest on blades of grass
sharpened by interplay of dark and light.

Today I breathed in deeply
chilled and effervescent air,
a heady sparkling wine
not to be served warm,
that invigorates the body
and elevates the mind;
outwardly also bathing in cold champagne
as it puckers and stiffens my fingers
and tingles on my scalp,
penetrating my brain.

Today I went for a walk;
my inside opened out,
the outside entered in,
and lovely, lovely peace got under my skin.

# Scotland

Introduce me to the patient
sister blossoming quietly, not
shouting about it, teeming
with fertile, multiplying
life.

Her clean, clear skin glows in
the clean, clear air, soft and
ruddy is the blush upon her
tender cheek.

So often veiled in grey and gauzy
cloak of modest moisture, lest we
dazzle with the colours of her
beauty.

For this maiden is not brash but
becoming.

Her self-contained and quiet
smile shimmers when the lifting
clouds reveal clear blue and
white, the sky that lets in thin
rarefied light on purple and
russet and green upon green upon
green upon grey upon green,
illuminated.

And as our lips part in
wonder, as we make that sharp
intake of breath, she drops
a welcoming curtsey of rosy
sunset.

# Lunan Beach
*Re-calibration*

Dappling – the interplay of light
Through light green leaves
Arching in welcome on approach,
The patterns of light
On intersecting ripples
As the waves come and go.

Diffracting – blades of light through
Shelves of overhanging pines
Create a sharpening lens.
The sand comes nearer
And recedes, looking down
Into waves around the feet.

Grounding – as the sea
Sucks away sand,
Sinking the feet in deeper,
Or as they plant
Into the soft, dry dunes,
Yielding and covering.

Perspective – looking out over the sea
To see a long, far horizon
Defined by the meeting of blues and grays,
Of water and of clouds,
Eyes caught by the arching
Of dolphins leaping and diving.

Settling – at the dunes
The marram grass has formed,
Sending out anchoring roots
Into a shape-shifting matrix
Hefted by wind and waves,
A bulwark set

Between the landward life
Where all is fixed and focussed,
Finite and purposeful,
And that creative shore
Where permanence
Shines through the insubstantial.

# Morden Park 7/9/21

September a shimmer of silver
on the underside of leaves
and in the air, the light
bright as before but thinner.

Not yet the rich painting
of autumn hues, glowing
in a slanting, fading light;
the colours here are summer's
but rarefied, less lush.

I can breathe here, the heat
carries a fresh chill,
harbinger of winter's
astringency.

I take in a deep breath
of new life, of adventuring.
Why does September always feel
Like a beginning?

# Ancient Oak

I squat on a log, a tree fairy
under a canopy of ancient oak.
A thick branch overhangs me.
How did it get that shape?
How does it hang there at such
an angle, its lowest leaves
Gently grazing the ground?

Dappled sunlight filters through
the curtain of leaves, some
translucent and alight,
leaves thicker and splaying,
spreading, the lower they get,
a green cascade surrounding
this inner space,
this magic circle of shade.

I would settle for growing old
if I could settle like this oak,
not defying gravity, but letting it
create a wide globe of protection,
a safe space, a shelter
for others, a curtain raised
for them to look through
as they try to frame
their world.

# Birthday Month

Serene September,
soft and green and
shining, when the
warmth and chill arrive
together, when the
hush after harvest
breathes repose.

I hope I was born
on such a day
of white gold sunlight,
filtered through light cloud
dappled and stretched
across a high wide sky

with the green fading
so there was no glare
when I opened my
eyes upon the world,
gentle to one so
sensitive to light.

# 65<sup>th</sup>. Birthday

What sort of a milestone is this?
One that says downhill
All the way from here?
Descending to a pleasant valley,
Staying near?
Cosy at journey's end
With feet up
In front of the fire?
Is there another path here?
One that will take me higher
And further – I want to explore
The places I couldn't go before,
Unreachable when earning my way,
Nurturing a family,
Furthering a career.
No dizzy heights or precipice,
Just a slow and steady climb
To a high and open place
Where I can find
Perspective
And a sense of the sublime.

I would like a long, slow, glorious sunset,
A light show in many acts
And colours, with clouds enough
To glow under a rainbow prism
Of light, as the sun's angle lengthens.
And when the shadow strengthens
May I be found
On an open hilltop
That seems to touch the sky,
So that it's just one short step
Into the sweet by and by.

# A Ride on a Speedboat

The definition of exhilaration,
It's quintessence.
Did I hear or feel
The synaesthetic roar
As we left slow shore
And soared in open water?
Was it the soundwaves
Or the vibrations
That set my eardrums buzzing,
As my ears picked out in colour
On this backdrop of intoxicating,
Mesmerising sound
The screech of a seagull
And the fat splash of waves
Hitting the side
At fifty miles an hour?

Salt set skin a-tingling
And tantalised the tongue;
Acupuncture of seaspray,
Fine needles sending joy
Piercing through the body,
As we rode full swells,
Bounced down into the troughs,
Splashed with more than spray,
Shaking with movement and laughter,
Shaken almost out of self
Into a stripe of speed and wind.

Flickering horizontals
Of grey, white, blue, green, brown
Catching the eye
Seeing too fast to focus.

Facing away from land
For a moment inhabiting
Nothing but ocean;
One surrounding element
To clarify existence.

It took a long time to land,
Ears still buzzing, eyes still glazed,
Body still feeling the motion,
Ecstasy still gripping the soul,
Finally grounded to earth
By the smells of fish sheds
And engine fuel, seaweed,
Fish and chips, and coffee.

# Better Felt Than Telt

Six weeks untouched by human hands.
Feels like I'm on another plan-
et, where the sense of touch has been cancelled, skin trembles to meet nothing,
fractions of a greeting:
a smile to see, a voice to hear,
but as for touch, nothing so near.

Turns out touch was not made for
inanimate objects: a cool floor,
a rough gate, warm stone wall in the sun or
smooth silk, the texture of velour.
Even a leaf or a blade of grass
fails to satisfy; let it pass.
I want a hug or a hand to clasp,
someone alive within my grasp,
shoulder to shoulder with my friend
on the sofa, not one at each end,
a smacking kiss or a peck on the cheek –
without all these my life is bleak.

For me to create a sense of community
I need to feel some close proximity,
and the words of a lover are an illusion
until they're confirmed by physical fusion.

Will I ever again complain
about a tube train,
pressed up against humanity,
smelling their breath,
wishing they hadn't
smoked that cigarette?

Forgive me for wanting
to keep my distance;
I'm so hungry now
for felt shared existence.

# Wells-next-the-sea

Sea breeze catches
a seagull, a skirt,
pink and white twirls,
sand hurled from a spade,
a flag, a kite
swooping and diving.

Catches snatches
of conversation,
laughter, calls, shouts,
dissipates
meaning and thought
into blissful blur.

Ripples the sea
into small waves
over the feet,
cooling and soothing,
washing and moving
our solid ground.

# Now the Day is Over
*a poem for Jack*

You would have loved
the shiny blue marble I found
when I dug down today
to plant a dahlia.
You wouldn't have chosen those,
unless it was for me
because I liked them;
maybe the purple lupin,
but not at those prices.
You would have gone
to the place you drove past last week,
where you bought cold drinks
and chatted to the owner,
and after half an hour
you would have known
the name of his daughter
and why he was worried about her.
You would have watered the garden tonight,
rotating two watering cans,
filling and pouring by turns,
just like I have done,
because I used to watch you.

You would have spotted the bat flitting past
as the sky grew darker,
shown me Venus the evening star
growing bigger and brighter.
You might have lingered in the doorway
before we closed the door against the night,
and put your arms around me
in the last romantic light of evening.
And then you would have turned,
turned on the light and put the kettle on:
"Nice cup of tea?"

And later, I would have lain beside you,
your back rising and falling with the breath,
that breath a sound as soothing as the sea,
waves rising and falling all night long,
and going on forever.

# Gentle Moods CD

I remember it like yesterday:
Held by your encircling arm,
My head upon your shoulder,
Warm,
Listening to this music,
While a candle flickered,
And we drifted off to sleep,
Safe.
'My heart will go on'
Finds another memory:
Singing our hearts out
At the karaoke
In Qingdao.
When the students asked us
To do this song the honours,
Did they know the story
Of the film?
Did they see Jack dying
And drifting away,
Leaving the heroine's heart
To go on?
Did they know survival
Apart from each other
Was really the subject
Of this song?
Could they see me lying here
With my memories and music,
Feeling the warmth and safety,
Alone?

## love was…

love was stomach-churning
butterflies inside
heart misses a beat
when I saw you in the street
unexpectedly
and this was only
three hours after you had left for work
after spending the night
together five thousand times

love was safe and steady
always ready
with a comforting hug
words of love
a refuge to hide
arms open wide
and always provide
unflinching support
someone on your side
who wasn't going anywhere

love was deep and satisfying
peaceful, belonging
knowing you were home
never quite alone
touching the core of me
anchoring my identity
and creative
making sweet, sweet music together
and out of that pleasure
creating children

love was tiring, demanding
exasperating
repeatedly weathering
misunderstanding
false landings
taking a stand on
different viewpoints
tensions, out of joint
working it out
commitment meeting compromise

love was energising
enabling, inspiring
encouraging ourselves
to be our best
egging us on to
another adventure
cheering us on
right up to
the finish line
every time

every time
until the last
finishing line

# Afterwards

Some people say
It's hardest in the morning
Finding a reason
To get out of bed
And start another disorientated day
But I say
It's hardest in the evening
Finding a reason to get into bed
Into that empty space
That used to hold embrace
Still, I manage to sleep well
Most days, these days
And when I don't
Well, there's always books…

# Memory

memory doesn't mind
the measurement of time
links without logic
flick of a switch
to random recreation

I can feel the hairs on your arm
your cool smooth leg
the safety of your
physicality
bigger than me

I can hear you singing
old revival hymns
in Welsh or Irish accents
hear you laughing
uncontrollably,
infectiously, unmistakeable
from the far side of the tent
located by laughter

I am lying dazed
receiving medical attention
watching you,
hearing you,
receive into the world
each child I have just birthed

I am sitting in the passenger seat
of the car, being taken
for a drive, I like to be
a passenger, I like to be
taken out

It was good to feel
safe like that.

# Note to the Care Home

Here's an apple pie
I made for Dad.
Cut him a big slice.
He likes it warm
But not soggy;
You must put it
In the oven,
Not the microwave.
Cover it with cream
Lavishly.

Make sure to tell him
The apples came
From the old tree
In his garden,
Where he built us
The tree house.
This might bring tears
To his eyes but
They will be the tears
Of warm memories.

And whatever
Superlatives
He might confer
On the pie,
Remind him that
Mum always made
The best ones.

# Mum and Dad

There was that magic moment, that
Window opening in the
Constricting confusion
Of two dementias clashing,
Always out of synch,
Like the train you just missed,
The lovers in the film
Who should have met but
They were in two cars passing
Each other in opposite
Directions, unknowing.

But there was that magic moment
In the bay window of the ward
Where they both arrived together
At the same place, the same time,
And a window to the memories of
Sixty-five years opened, and I saw
The settling in each other's
Company, next to the person
Who makes you feel alright
Just by being there,
Whose hug settles your heart.

Two heads leaning together,
Satisfaction shared
In whatever sweet nothings
They were murmuring to each other,
Striking a hope of true love
Into every heart that saw them,
A yearning for love lost,
Or for some, love never found.
She, his treasure; he, her prize,
Replete with benedictions
In each other's eyes.

And even now, he is that
Presence, who drifts in and out of
Her room in the care home,
Wandering in and staying
For three hours, proffering biscuits,
Wandering out and forgetting
To come back, until she cries out
His name, that presence
Who will leave a gaping hole
In the centre of her heart
If he does not return.

# Anger

If I met COVID
In the street,
I'd smack it in the mouth, break
Every one of its teeth.
I'd shake it by the shoulders,
And shove it to the ground,
Making sure its head hit the paving stones
With a splintering, shattering sound.

Because COVID showed no mercy:
It took the fragile threads
Of my father's slanted Alzheimer's mind
And stirred them about in his head,
Until everything was upsidedown
And nothing would connect,
So he couldn't take his shoes off
Or get out of his bed.

And when he tried, it wrestled him,
Threw him to the floor,
Bruised him hard and broke his bones,
So he couldn't get about any more.
And then it stole his swallow
So he couldn't eat or drink.
It sucked away his strength
Until he began to sink.

I'd wear my heavy walking boots
And boot it in the balls
Again and again and again and again
Until it lost all ability to spawn.
Then I'd trample over and over
On its cruel and ugly face
Until any leering grin of victory
Was as far away as outer space.

Does that sound cruel? It's nothing
To the cruelty COVID deals,
Separating dying relatives
With no regard to how they feel,
Writing us a story
That's full of grieving tears,
Where my last hug of my father's lifeless body
Was the first time I'd hugged him for a year.

# Undoing

Crumpled in on yourself
Experience folded and wrinkled
More than the blanket
That you clutch with grasping fingers
More than the fragile skin
Stretched on your withered frame
Contracted and foetal
The presentable is lost
In the imploded layers
That side you showed the world
Inner folds turned outwards
Exposing random fragments
Flashes of brilliance or fears
Rooted deeply in telescopic years.

Where is Mum? And John?
Why have they left you?
He was here a moment ago
Dancing the rumba so
Why do you feel alone?
Yesterday you spoke
In phrases of French
Gave a German greeting
And shopped for groceries
In Croydon, Surrey Street
On a Saturday afternoon.

Why do they feed you baby food
And bring so many pills
When swallowing exhausts you?
Can't they see you have so much to do?
You are so deeply tired
Yet even as you close
Your heavy eyelids
You are always haunted by
That sense of something needing to be done
That something needing doing
Even as you are dismantled
Disordered, and undone.

# Stop

The brass clock on the wall is frozen
At six fifty-three and forty seconds,
AM or PM, I don't know.
Next to the clock face a springbok frozen
In mid-leap jumps in relief
Over ground where it will never land,
And soon you too will,
Like the springbok clock, stop.

# Therapy

Where does it hurt?
Let's see where it's broken.
Uncover that wound,
Don't leave it unspoken:
A full reveal,
Not just a token.
What's in the box?
Don't leave it unopened.

Take off the lid,
I know it smells.
Pick up the stone,
Unblock the wells.
Let feelings out
From prison cells,
Down in the depths
Where memory dwells.

Deep in the woods,
What will you find
In the dark corners
Of your mind?
All of the pain
That got left behind
When you ran from fear
And forgot to be kind.

Take it all with you
Into your day,
The pain that you dropped
Along the way.
Imperfection
Is here to stay,
Must be accepted,
Won't go away.

Things that are hidden
Will grow and grow;
You must get them out
To let them go.
If you never dig,
You'll never know
Gems also glitter
In the mine below.

Whatever has happened,
You can't negate
The savage twists
And turns of fate,
But you have the power
To negotiate
Within yourself,
To navigate
To somewhere safe.
It's not too late
To accept each part
Of your broken state,
To hold it there,
To integrate.

# An Invitation

Detach the linchpin from its lock-in,
Send it into lockdown instead;
Weigh the anchor that has been firmly holding
Location for the living and the dead;
Splinter the springboard into matchwood,
With the imprints of the feet that have gone far;
Let the launchpad be dismantled
Which powered them forth, aiming for the stars.

You have scattered abroad your gift of language,
Enabled other voices all around;
You have celebrated their expression,
But have you ever listened to the sound
Of your own voice? There. You have gone silent.
Do you even know what you want to say?
Would you like to stop and think and leave a message?
Send out your voice? You can. Will you? You may.

# Not Allowed

I cannot remember the occasion,
The season, day, the hour, the month, the year.
All I know is that 'You are not allowed'
Are words I simply cannot bear to hear.

I do not know the thing that was denied me,
As dear as love or trivial as a snack,
But the freedom to ask for what I want
Is something that I definitely lack.

I learnt so very early not to ask
For credit, as refusal can offend,
And now I am full of apologies
If I would like a favour from a friend.

'Needy' became a silent badge of shame
Because I ought to be self-sufficient,
But if we were made for relationship
What made me think I had to be so different?

This year I started to 'allow myself',
I started to 'give myself permission'
But how would it be if I 'went for it'
Not stopping to consider such decisions?

How would it be if the Shadow didn't fall
Between the idea and the action?
Running through open doors, lights set at green,
Embracing life's lovely invitation.

# Organic

Last year I dug up roots,
Planted seeds of truth,
Wrestled underground
With every sub- and super-
Structure that I found.

Planted and tended,
Creativity flourished:
Pumpkins and poems,
Lilies and lettuces,
Flowers and fruit
Kindling joy and freedom
Of new life
With every picture, word and tune.

This year I continued clearing weeds,
Though less convincing,
Roots not so deep,
Loosening freely
From the well-dug earth.
Still, they troubled me.

Growth arrived with stealth.
Who can say which seed
Germinated, unbidden,
The moment of conception hidden
Until that instant when
The new life growing
Inside you moves,
Removing doubt.
No option now
But to let it keep on growing
Until the day when it comes out
Into the world.

And so I know
On this green and peaceful morning,
Seated under an ancient oak,
That I have grown up, quietly,
Secretly, organically,
Almost without noticing,
By life, not by decision,
By truth and not by artifice,
Into the rest
Of who I am.

# Worship

Let me sing you a symphony,
Every part of me
An instrument adding to the harmony,
A crescendo like the one you create
At the beginning of every day
When you paint
The moving light show of the dawn.
Let rhythm and rhyme
Make patterns in time,
Powerful like the moving of the tides,
Ebbing and flowing like music,
Taking it high, taking it low;
Let my song with glory glow,
Moving out into the great expanse
Of who you are.

A symphony
Is what I want to sing you
But sometimes
A few simple notes are needed
Or a wordless unmusical groan,
Because you want to inhabit
The quiet whisper of peace,
The wrenching gasp of sorrow,
And the sublime soaring
Of my song.

# Formation

Before it became a jewel
in a crown, this diamond was
superheated and subjected
to tremendous force, under
pressure, under a hundred
miles of rock, and if the heat
was hot like the heat
of the sun, and the
pressure was the weight
of the whole world, then the
time taken was so very slow
and long, the years a
number followed by many
zeroes. And before this
diamond could reflect
the light, it was ejected
convulsively in molten
streams of lava, pouring out
from a volcano; cooled and
solidified, waiting for the
pick-axe and the dynamite,
the cutting and the shaping.

And this I think is how
hope is formed, because
if not, what is this
unyielding solid speck
I cannot let go of
in the darkness, heat and
heaviness, under repeated
tonnages, that travels
with me in the rush of
boiling lava, the
hardening and then the
mining, in the sharpness
of cutting and the
artistry of setting, this
diamond that I know
will sparkle when its
weighty treasure catches
the light?

# From the Depths I Cry to You

God of the God-particle,
Holding all things together
By the Higgs-Bosun word of Your power,
Hold me together;
I am weary of catching fragments,
Losing the battle against
The entropy that makes me fall apart.

Author of Grand Narrative,
Tell my story;
My petits recits
Run into dead ends daily;
Their banality appals me,
As the many wire-strong threads
Slip through my bleeding fingers.
I cannot even hold them:
To weave them together
Is not within my art.

Master of Mathematics,
Stringing together chaos theory,
Former of fractals,
Pattern upon pattern
Reductio ad minisculum,
Multiplier of life through
Fibonacci numbers,
Balancer of the Golden Ratio,
Make something beautiful
Of the fractured disorder
Of my heart.

# Vulnerable

a trembling bird resting
in the hollow of Your hand
until the convulsing waves
of sorrow and alarm
are comforted

a candle flame
clinging to its last flicker,
drowning in its melted detritus,
cupped by Your sheltering hand,
revived by the gentlest exhalation
of Your breath

a tiny shoot
that dared to look at February
and now, exposed, can only grow
and not draw back,
Your tear that falls upon it
hot with love
and rich in nutrients

my anxious heart seeking
the Everlasting Arms

# Held

"Lean in," He said.
It was warm there,
A quiet shelter
Out of the wind.

"Lean harder," He said
As the ground began to quake,
"This rock is solid,
Immovable." It was.

Then the ground began to crumble
But I didn't feel it fall away
From underneath my feet,
Scooped up in strong arms and carried.

My arms fastened
About Your neck,
My head resting
On Your shoulder,
My tears falling
As Your heartbeat
Calibrates my own
To the rhythm of Your love,
Rising and falling
With heaven's breath.

# This Is My Story

Between a rock and a hard place,
That's the place I've been wandering in,
Because when You kicked away the props
I didn't know where to begin.

Relationships, location
Suddenly far away,
Roles and occupations
No longer for today,
Complete disorientation
So I couldn't find my way,
Distress and dislocation
The order of the day.
And in this situation, to my great consternation,
The health of body and mind gave way.

When I started falling
I didn't know where I would land,
And as I suffer from vertigo
It seemed like a challenging plan,
But all I could think of to do was let go
And fall into Your hands,
And I was caught and I was fought for
By the rock whose face I recognised
As I came to a standstill
And on whose bedrock I still stand.

A rock that when struck releases
A fountain of life-giving grace,
A rock that when cleft uncovers
The safest hiding place.
A rock that is rock bottom
So there's nowhere else to drop,
A rock I thought I already knew
Before You kicked away the props.

To be honest, at the time,
It felt like a kick in the teeth,
Like the whole floor, not only the rug,
Being pulled from under my feet.
But the prize, the star prize in the wilderness,
The greatest, the most life-giving, the best,
Face to face in the wilderness,
Worth every strain and every stress,
Is knowing more securely
The solid rock beneath.

# Other excellent titles from London Poetry Books

Sibling Ribaldries,
Rather Rude Rhymes.                Nicky & Heather Sullivan
Joy Fear and F—k It.               Ant Smith
There is a Tune.                   Cathy Flower
Dark Matter.                       Amy Neilson Smith
Pathways.                          Anne Gaelan
The Mirrors of Thespis.
Pocket Full of Whispers
Art Square Look & Stare.
Skyhigh Down to Ground.
Down Ghost Lane                    Keith Bray
English is a Foreign Language.
Outside in musin on life,
As an Autistic Poet.               Alain English
Swimming with Endorphins.          Fran Isherwood
Ooetry.                            Wendy Young
Going with the Flow.
Making it Verse.
Rhymes for the Times.              Habiba Hrida
I'm not here for your,
Entertainment.                     Tara Fleur
Life and Hope.
Death Suicide Despair,
Poetry.                            Jason Harris
Twisted and Chewed.                Shaun Rivers
In the Name of the Flesh.          Ernesto Sarezale

L - #0147 - 021122 - C0 - 210/148/4 - PB - DID3412726